The Importance of the Blood of Jesus Christ

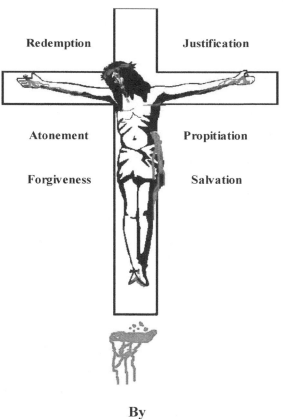

Redemption　　Justification

Atonement　　Propitiation

Forgiveness　　Salvation

By
Robert R. Breaker III

The Importance of the Blood of Jesus Christ
(especially in our age of apostasy)

By

Robert R. Breaker III

"Woe unto the man that tramples upon the blood of Christ, and treats it as an unholy thing! Alas! I fear that many are doing so at this hour, not only among the outside world, but among those who profess and call themselves Christians."
— *Charles Hadden Spurgeon*

The Importance of the Blood of Jesus Christ

Written by

Robert R. Breaker III

1st Edition

© 2008

All rights reserved.

ISBN-13: 978-1463762179

ISBN-10: 1463762178

All Scripture quoted in this work is from the *Authorized* King James Bible.

THE IMPORTANCE OF THE BLOOD:

We are *justified* by His Blood (Rom. 5:9)

We have *redemption* through His Blood (Eph. 1:7)

We have *forgiveness of sins* by His Blood (Col. 1:14)

We are *made nigh* to God by His Blood (Eph. 2:13)

We have *peace* through His Blood (Col. 1:20)

We have a *purged conscience* through His Blood (Heb. 9:4)

We have *boldness* through His Blood (Heb. 10:19)

We are *sanctified* by His Blood (Heb. 10:29)

We are *cleansed* by His Blood (1 John 1:7)

We are *washed from our sin* by His own Blood (Rev. 1:5)

We *overcome the accuser* by His Blood (Rev. 12:11)

Introduction

If there is one thing missing in Modern Christianity it is *the Blood* of the Lord Jesus Christ. Far too many Christians think that it doesn't need to be mentioned, as it might be *"offensive"* to the lost, dying world. Instead of preaching the wounded, beaten, crucified Christ that shed his own precious blood for the sins of mankind, they teach a milksop, non-offensive, sugar-coated gospel of *commitment* and *dedication*, instructing sinners to simply, *"Give their life to God,"* or, *"Ask Him into their heart."*

But this completely omits the blood sacrifice of Jesus, and makes salvation dependent upon what one *DOES*, rather than what Jesus, in his infinite love and mercy, *DID* for mankind!

Christianity has come a long way from its humble beginnings. It took root and flourished because men like the apostles rigidly preached the vicarious substitutionary blood atonement, death, burial, and resurrection of Jesus Christ under the power and influence of the Holy Ghost. They not only stressed salvation through *faith in the shed blood of Jesus*, but were willing to die for their Lord if need be, *shedding their own blood* for the cause of Christ. Because of their testimony, countless millions of souls came to Christ Jesus alone for salvation, many of them also dying as martyrs for Him who loved them enough to die for their sins.

But my how times have changed! Nowadays, most Christians aren't willing to *live* for Jesus, much less *die* for him! They don't desire to tell the gory, blood-stained Gospel that saves sinners and converts the soul. They'd rather spread a carnal, *social gospel* that changes one outwardly, instead of the *Substitutionary Gospel* of Christ's atonement.

Christianity today has become portrayed as a polished, cultured, sophisticated society of intellectuals who are known by their *fair speeches* (Rom. 16:18) to captivate the hearer and gain an awe of elegance. But this is not the Christianity of days gone by! It used to be when speaking of Christianity, many referred to it as *That Old Slaughter House Religion*. Why? Because they knew it was BLOODY!

It appears to me that modern Christianity has assumed an effeminate character (especially with so many *women preachers* everywhere), and this is the main reason for the omission and negligence of preaching the true Biblical Gospel of Christ's shedding His blood for the sins of the world.

Gone are the old-time, manly preachers who hollered, spat, shout, and screamed against sin, while exalting the bleeding Saviour for all to see and admire. It's hard to find any real men anymore who will rear back and let 'er rip, preaching until their throats bleed, like the immortal George Whitefield.

Instead, most modern-day ministers are panty-laced drones spit out of Sissy Factories, called Fundamental Colleges, like robots on an assembly line. As they were trained, they behave with *tact* and *genteelness*, striving to present the gospel in a *pleasing fashion*, while working towards *the goal of non-offensiveness* to the hearer. They are effeminate in their mannerisms and portray Jesus as a *compassionate mother*, ready with arms open to accept all who simply *acknowledge Him*, rather than depicting Him as THE MAN CHRIST JESUS (2 Tim. 2:5), whose wrath abides on those who deny *His atonement* (John 3:36).

The characteristics of the female species are not hard to miss. They are squeamish, and don't like the sight of blood, or even hearing about it. Women as a whole just don't like *gross things*. So too these attributes are found among finicky modernists and apostates who call themselves Christians. Talking about blood offends them and leaves them nauseous and queasy. Thus, they speak only of *love* and *grace*, not *sacrifice* and *atonement*.

Instead of preaching the Gospel they only "share" it. Instead of giving sermons, they "speak at sessions." Instead of crying aloud against sin, they give "devotional talks." Instead of pointing to Christ crucified, they only "praise his passion."

They have turned Christianity into a feminine religion, and have changed sound Biblical terms into cordial, psychological expressions designed to make people *feel good about themselves*, instead of *bad for their sins* which put Jesus on the cross. In short, Modern day Christianity is guilty of preaching a BLOOD-LESS GOSPEL!

For this very reason, the blood of Jesus Christ has lost it's importance to so many. However, to God it's just as important as it ever was!

This booklet is written to show you the importance of the precious blood of Christ. Though many would like to omit it, and still claim they are Christians, I WILL PROVE THROUGH THE REST OF THIS WORK THAT IT'S IMPOSSIBLE TO EVEN BE A CHRISTIAN WITHOUT TRUSTING SOLELY IN THE PRECIOUS SHED BLOOD OF JESUS CHRIST. That's how important it is!

WHAT IS BLOOD AND WHERE DOES IT COME FROM?

There is probably no other liquid in the world as amazing as blood. According to Robert Coleman, "Every cubic millimeter of the blood—a speck the size of a pin head—has in it approximately 5,500,000 living cells. These cells live from 110 to 120 days. To replenish those cells which have fulfilled their life function, the body manufactures almost 2,000,000 new cells every second." [1] This is simply astounding!

Doctor M.R. DeHaan tells us that blood consists of two parts—**plasma**, a colorless liquid in which are suspended the various cellular elements and chemicals, and **platelets**, thin transparent cells. These platelets are made up of three types, which include: the **erythrocytes**, or red blood cells which carry oxygen, the **leucocytes**, which help combat infection, and the **antibodies** which work in preventing disease. [2]

But even with all the above mentioned medical knowledge about man's blood, Dr. DeHaan admits the following, "Man has learned a great deal about blood since the discovery of the microscope...although much is still a mystery." [3]

It is true, science has discovered much about what blood is, and what it's made of, but they have yet to explain the most important thing—ITS ORGIN. Thus, in order to understand the importance of the Blood of Jesus Christ, we must first understand what blood is and where it came from.

If the theory of Evolution is correct (and it most certainly is not according to the Bible), it gives us absolutely NO EXPLANATION WHATSOEVER for how blood came into existence. Blood did not evolve, it could not. Blood had to be created.

God denying, secular evolutionists want us to believe that millions of years ago, rain falling on rocks produced life. Then after millions of years, single-celled organisms slowly turned into multi-celled creatures, each one moving a little higher up on the food chain. Yet in this ridiculous theory, the question stands out like a sore thumb, *"Where does blood come from?"*

For the simple fact is that no bacteria, single-celled organism, amoeba, or virus has blood! Where then did blood enter the picture? Modern science has no answer. They simply do not know.

We must then turn to the Bible, for it's only there that we find the origin of blood.

CHAPTER ONE
THE ORIGIN OF BLOOD

According to the Bible, God created man (Gen. 1:27), and put him in a garden (Gen. 2:8), to dress and keep it (Gen. 2:15). God then commanded the man to eat of any tree that he so desired except for the forbidden tree of *the knowledge of good and evil* (Gen 2:16,17), for if he ate of that tree, he would die (Gen. 2:18).

We all know what happened next. God created the woman, and Satan tricked her into eating from the forbidden tree (Gen. 3:1-6). When she did, she died spiritually. Adam also ate, and the history of mankind's fallen, sinful nature flooded history books thereafter.

What was this forbidden tree? Many claim it was an *apple*. But the Scriptures do not tell us this. No, the golden apple story comes from ancient Greek Mythology. [4]

Although the exact fruit on the tree of the knowledge of good and evil is left unstated in the word of God, the Bible hints that it most likely was a *grape*, and that man's blood came from the juice of this fruit (or one very much like it).

There are numerous passages to prove this. For example, in Deuteronomy 32:14, we read the words, "**the PURE BLOOD of the grape.**" Here *grape juice* is called *blood*.

In Genesis 49:11, we read about someone that "**washed his garments in wine...his clothes in THE BLOOD OF GRAPES.**" Again wine, or grape juice, is likened unto blood.

Ezekiel 19:10 says, "**Thy mother is like A VINE IN THY BLOOD, planted by the waters: she was fruitful and full of branches by reason of many waters.**" Here the grape vine is equated with blood.

Right off the bat, someone would be quick to counter this notion with "*But grapes don't grow in trees, they grow on vines!"* However, the Bible always speaks of the grape vine as a TREE, as seen in the following verses:

All the days of his separation shall he eat nothing that is made of the <u>vine tree</u>, from the kernels even to the husk.
 - Numbers 6:4

Son of man, What is the <u>vine tree</u> more than any tree, *or than* a branch which is among the trees of the forest?
 - Ezekiel 15:2

Therefore thus saith the Lord GOD; As the <u>vine tree</u> among the trees of the forest, which I have given to the fire for fuel, so will I give the inhabitants of Jerusalem.
 - Ezekiel 15:6

Biblically, grapes grow on vine *trees*. Could the tree of the knowledge of good and evil have been a grape tree? And could Adam and Eve have gotten their blood from eating this "forbidden fruit?" Let us explore the possibility.

Grape juice is chemically very close to human blood. Not only in color, but in consistency and properties. In fact some doctors theorize that if all of a person's blood is removed and replaced with only pure 100% grape juice, their body would still function properly. This remains to be tested and proven, but one thing is for sure: the only *forbidden fruit* in the Bible is THE GRAPE, forbidden to the sect of the Nazarites in Numbers 6:3-4.

In the Garden of Eden, the Bible describes three different trees. First, we encounter *the tree of the knowledge of good and evil* (Gen. 2:9 and 17). Next, we see *the tree of life* (Genesis 2:9), and finally we find *a fig tree* (which represents man's self righteousness), which Adam and Eve used to cover their nakedness after their sin (Gen. 3:7).

With this in mind, we have an interesting coincidence (if not sound Bible truth) by studying the rest of the Bible. For many times the *fig*, the *grape*, and the *olive* tree are all mentioned together in scripture. Some references include: Deut. 8:8, Judges 9;8-15, 2 Kings 18:30-32, Amos 4:9, Haggai 2:19, and James 3:12.

If the fruit of *the tree of the knowledge of good and evil* was a *grape*, and *the tree of life* was an *olive* tree (olive oil is a type of the Holy Spirit in the Bible, who seals the believer and gives him *eternal life*), these passages would then do well to prove that the three trees mentioned in the garden of Eden in the first three chapters of Genesis are the *grape, olive,* and *fig*.

Apart from the scriptures pointing to the grape being the tree of the knowledge of good and evil, and being the origin of man's blood, let us look at the etymology of the word Adam—the first man—for his name holds within itself an interesting discovery.

The word ADAM in Hebrew is אדם. It literally means *reddish* or *ruddy*, or in it's Pual participle form, *made or dyed red*.[5]

However, if someone separates the word in Hebrew into two words (א and דם or *A* and *Dam*), an interesting word picture unfolds. The word "Dam" in Hebrew is the word for *blood*. And the "A" can be used as the interrogative *where?*[6]

In English, there are times when we use the letter "a" in front of a word as a negation. For example, *Muse* means to think. *A-muse* means to not think. Isn't it interesting that the word *Adam* means *red*, the color of blood. And if you break the word into two Hebrew words, you get the question, *"Where's blood?"* Or in English the statement *"No blood."*

In other words, it appears that Adam was created *without blood*. But when he fell, he then became *reddish*, and his body's circulatory system became one of thick, rich blood when he ate of the forbidden fruit.

For those who find this too far fetched, let's look at the following verses which teach that drinking blood (taking it orally, like Adam took the fruit orally) is forbidden in the Bible.

Before the law of Moses, in Genesis 9:4, we find a command for men to not eat blood. *Under the law*, in Leviticus 17:12, men again are instructed not to eat blood. And *after the law*, in the period of the church age (of which we are in today), we read in Acts 15:29 that Christians should abstain from blood. Other references against the drinking of blood are: Deut. 12:23, Lev. 3:17; 7:26,17 and 19:26.

God demands that men not drink or eat blood. Why? Could it be because man received his blood by the method of *EATING* the forbidden fruit? If one is a Bible Believer, he has no other alternative but believe this is so.

When Adam took of the forbidden fruit, he fell. He died *spiritually*, and brought upon himself the curse of dying *physically* later. He changed from an *immortal* to an *mortal* being cursed with corrupt, sinful blood.

Some believe that Adam before the fall had only a water circulatory system without blood. Although the scriptures do not dogmatically state this to be so, they do allude to this idea through the following examples.

The first miracle in the Old Testament was Moses turning *water* into *blood* in Exodus 4:9. Similarly, the first miracle in the New Testament was Jesus turning *water* into *wine* (a type of blood) in John 2:1-10.

When Jesus died on the Cross, the Bible tells us in John 19:34, that forthwith out came *water* and *blood*. And in 2 Samuel 23:17 and 1 Chronicles 11:19, David likens the *water* that his soldiers brought him to drink unto the *blood* of the men that jeopardized their lives to bring it to him.

Whether Adam had a water circulatory system to start with or not is subject to debate. However, that Adam received blood is a fact. And the Bible tells us that this blood in Adam is what gave him his *physical life*.

In Leviticus 17:14 we read:

For *it is* the life of all flesh; the blood of it *is* for the life thereof: therefore I said unto the children of

Israel, Ye shall eat the blood of no manner of flesh: for the life of all flesh *is* the blood thereof: whosoever eateth it shall be cut off.

This verse states that the *life* of man's flesh is his *blood*. Blood equals life and life equals blood. Without blood, man can not even be a living creature. In order to be alive and reading this, you have to have blood coursing through your veins!

M.R. DeHaan says on this subject, *"Life, that mysterious something which scientists have never yet been able to define or fathom, is said by God to be in the blood of the flesh, so that there can be no life without the blood."* [7]

Thus, according to the Bible, life and blood started with God, and are not the product of *evolution*, rather the *innovation* of the Creator.

THE TWO THEORIES OF HOW BLOOD WAS MADE

Now let us discuss exactly how blood came into being. There are two theories about this. They are:

1. God created man with blood in him already.

2. Man's sin and disobedience in eating the forbidden fruit changed his body's circulatory system into one of blood.

The theory that God himself created man with blood in him has been perpetuated by Doctor M.R. Dehaan. He attributes blood to God's *direct creation*, when he says, *"The breath of God put something in man that made him ALIVE. That something was blood. It must have been. It could be nothing else: for we have already shown that the life of the flesh is in the blood and so when life was added by the breath of God, He imparted blood to that lump of clay in the shape of a man, and man became a living soul. Adam's body was of the ground. His blood was the separate gift of God..."* [8]

This theory says that God himself made blood and put it in man. However, this creates a problem. Man's blood is tainted, sinful, and corrupt. And we know that God does not make junk! He makes things correctly!

This brings us to our second theory; how God made man with a water circulatory system, but he fell and his fall produced sinful, corrupt blood.

According to this theory, man's blood is his *physical life*. Because he is sinful and fallen, man will not live forever. He has a problem with his blood. DeHaan continues, *"Remember that the life is in the blood, and so if man must die it is because there is death in the blood. Although we do not know the nature of the fruit of the tree of knowledge of good and evil, we do know that the eating of it caused 'blood poisoning' and resulted in death... So potent was this poison that six thousand years after, all who are related to Adam by human birth still succumb to that poison of sin which is carried in some way in the blood."* [9]

All men and women born into the world today are born into a life of suffering; full of heartaches, pain, and death. And every man woman and child on this earth will someday die because of his sinful, corrupt blood.

These are the two theories. One states that God made blood, but we know that God did not make it *corrupt* and *sinful*. The more probable answer then, is that God made Adam with a water circulatory system, and by eating the forbidden fruit, the grape (or grape-like fruit), Adam's body underwent a change, which corrupted his pure circulatory system. Rich, red liquid then coursed through his veins, corrupting his entire body, condemning him and eventually killing him, and his entire race.

Hebrews 9:27 tells us, **"And as it is appointed unto men once to die, but after this the judgment."**

All human beings are subject to death because of Adam's sin. And that sin affected the blood. *Sin* was the cause, *blood* is the product, and *death* is the impending condemnation.

Our life is therefore dependent upon blood. Without blood, we have no physical life. However, our blood is contaminated. It's polluted. For this, we CANNOT live forever. Life for a human being is only temporal, thanks to Adam.

In contrast, the blood of the Lord Jesus Christ is much different. It is sinless, precious blood. Acts 20:28 calls it "GOD'S BLOOD."

And, my how wondrous the Biblical story! The great God of heaven, in his infinite mercy and grace came down into this world and lived for thirty-three years without sinning one time. Then, on Golgotha's bloody hillside, He willingly shed His own sinless, divine blood on the cross of Calvary to pay for the sins of mankind. Through this act of mercy, He gave to humanity the way to obtain eternal life. They can have a spiritual blood transfusion!

For the Bible teaches that through faith in the blood of Jesus Christ, eternal life is offered to all who willingly accept His sacrifice of shed blood! Instead of *temporal life* with corrupt blood, man can have eternal, *spiritual life* through the precious blood of God himself!

How important is the divine blood of Jesus Christ!

CHAPTER TWO
FORGIVENESS BY THE SHEDDING OF BLOOD

Blood Sacrifices for Atonement of Sins in the Old Testament

"And almost all things are by the law purged with blood; and without shedding of blood is no remission."
- Hebrews 9:22

This verse states that without blood, there can be NO REMISSION OF SIN! This is why blood is so important. God has always demanded a blood sacrifice for man's sin. And without blood, no sins can be forgiven! As revolting and ghastly as this might sound, only a messy, bloody sacrifice can remit the sins of man before a holy and righteous God.

In the Old Testament, the remission of sins has always been dependent upon the bloody sacrifice of an animal. In the very first book of the Bible, we find God himself killing a poor innocent lamb for Adam and Eve and clothing them in its skin (Gen. 3:21).

We then encounter Abel in Genesis chapter four offering up one of the sheep from his flock to God, slaying it as a blood sacrifice, and the Lord had respect unto him for it (Genesis 4:4).

In Genesis 22:13, we discover Abraham offering up a ram to God as a sacrificial burnt offering. Jacob also sacrifices in Genesis 31:54. And the twelve tribes of Israel follow suit throughout the entire Old Testament.

In Exodus, we read about the Passover, in which the Children of Israel sacrificed lambs and applied the blood on their door posts to keep the destroyer from killing their first born. When he saw the blood, he *passed over* them (Exodus 12:13).

Under the law of Moses, sacrifices were commanded, and an entire priest class, the Levites, were given the work of offering up blood to God upon the altar.

In the time of Joshua, we find Israel offering animal sacrifices (Joshua 8:30-32), and also during the time of the Judges (Judges 2:5).

Further, we read of the sacrifices offered by Elkanah (1 Sam. 1:1-3), Samuel (1 Sam. 16:2-5), David (2 Sam. 24:25), Solomon (I Kings 8:63), Ezra (Ezra 4:2), Job (Job 1:5), Elijah (1 Kings 18:36-39) and more. The Entire Old Testament is full of blood sacrifices!

Of the exact number of sacrifices offered in the Old Testament, it's impossible to count. One author gives us an idea when he says, *"the official public sacrifices prescribed by the law would number 1,273 per year (Numbers 28;1-29,39). If regularly observed, this would amount to almost 2,000,000 from Moses to Christ, apart from the countless millions of unnumbered individual offerings and additional public sacrifices."* [10]

However many sacrifices offered, one thing is certain—blood poured profusely in the Old Testament to remit man's sins!

The One Effectual Sacrifice of Christ Jesus in the New Testament

In the New Testament, forgiveness of sins is no longer dependent upon *man's sacrificing* of lambs, but upon *God's sacrificing himself for man* as the Lamb of God (John 1:29)—the ultimate blood sacrifice to pay the sin debt for all.

Instead of temporal *remission*, the blood of Jesus gives eternal *redemption*. Hebrews 9:12 clearly states, **"Neither by the blood of goats and calves, but by his own blood he entered in once into the holy place, having obtained eternal redemption** *for us."*

According to the Bible, the work of salvation is entirely finished, and an earthly, mortal priest is no longer needed, for in Hebrews 10:10-12 we read:

By the which will we are sanctified through the offering of the body of Jesus Christ ONCE FOR ALL. And every priest standeth daily ministering and offering oftentimes the same sacrifices, which can never take away sins: But this man, after he had offered **ONE SACRIFICE FOR SINS FOR EVER, sat down on the right hand of God.**

Jesus Christ offered His own blood to God in our stead. He died for our sins and became the ultimate sacrifice for the sins of the whole world!

Both the Old and New Testaments were sealed with blood. In Hebrews 9:15-20 we read:

15 And **for this cause he is the mediator of the new testament**, that by means of death, for the redemption of the transgressions *that were* under the first testament, they which are called might receive the promise of eternal inheritance. 16 **For where a testament *is*, there must also of necessity be the death of the testator.** 17 For a testament *is* of force after men are dead: otherwise it is of no strength at all while the testator liveth. 18 **Whereupon neither the first *testament* was dedicated without blood.** 19 For when Moses had spoken every precept to all the people according to the law, he took the blood of calves and of goats, with water, and scarlet wool, and hyssop, and sprinkled both the book, and all the people, 20 Saying, This *is* the blood of the testament which God hath enjoined unto you.

A Testament is what's read when someone dies. When God put Israel under the law, the Bible says that sacrifice was made, and Moses applied the blood of that sacrificed animal to the priest's right ear, right finger, and right toe, and around the altar (Exodus 29:20; Levi. 8:23,24). This started the *first Testament*.

When Jesus died, starting the *New Testament*, He in like manner was covered in blood (His own), and after He rose again, the Bible tells us that in His office as High Priest, He took His blood up to the mercy seat in heaven, and offered it there to God (Heb. 9:21-26) on our behalf.

Jesus is the ultimate and final sacrifice for the sins of mankind *once and for all*! (Heb. 10:10-12) Today, no more sacrifices are needed!

Now, Jesus sits on the right hand of the throne of God (Heb. 12:2). And the only way to get to God is through the BLOOD SACRIFICE of Jesus Christ. A sinner must come to God through *His blood*.

Hebrews 10:19 says, **"Having therefore, brethren, boldness to enter into the holiest by the blood of Jesus."**

THIS IS WHY THE SHED BLOOD OF JESUS CHRIST IS SO IMPORTANT. THERE'S SIMPLY NO ACCESS TO HEAVEN WITHOUT IT!

The Gospel of Blood

The Gospel is found in 1 Corinthians 15:1-4:

1 Moreover, brethren, I declare unto you the gospel which I preached unto you, which also ye have received, and wherein ye stand; 2 By which also ye are saved, if ye keep in memory what I preached unto you, unless ye have believed in vain. 3 For I delivered unto you first of all that which I also received, how that Christ died for our sins according to the scriptures; 4 And that he was buried, and that he rose again the third day according to the scriptures:

The Gospel has five parts:

1. *Christ died*
2. *For our sins*
3. *Was buried*
4. *Rose Again*
5. *According to the scriptures.*

The blood of Jesus is found in all five of these elements and is an integral part of the Gospel, interweaving and interlocking it together. Let us look at each part.

Christ died. Christ bore *five bleeding wounds* in his *hands, feet, head, back*, and *side* as He died. The day they crucified Jesus on that old rugged cross, He was stripped, beaten, prodded, whipped, nailed, pierced, and stuck with thorns. He suffered immense pain and anguish as man's depravity came to fruition and crucified the Lord of Glory. Yet, Jesus willingly shed every drop of blood in His body for you and me!

What a bloody sight our Lord must have been. Isaiah 52:14 tells us, **"...many were astonied...his visage was so marred more than any man, and his form more than the**

sons of men." He was so abused, He was barely recognizable. He was nothing but a bloody pulp of a man. My how the blood must have poured!

For our sins. The Lord Jesus not only shed every drop of blood on Calvary but He did so for us bloodthirsty and evil sinners. Isa. 1:18 equates man's sin with blood, when it says, "**Come now, and let us reason together, saith the LORD: though your sins be as scarlet, they shall be as white as snow; though they be red like crimson, they shall be as wool.**"

Man is bloody. By his very nature he's cruel, and vile. That's why he must be born again. But God reasons with him. He tells him that even though his sins are as the color of rich, red blood, God is willing to cleanse a man and make him as white as snow. All God demands is for man to accept the finished sacrifice of Jesus Christ by faith.

Was buried. Jesus was entombed in the same ground in which he shed His blood. Further, when Jesus died on the cross, His blood spilt unto the very ground that Abel's blood spilled nearly four thousand years earlier.

When Abel's blood was shed, God says it spoke to Him, for in Genesis 4:10 we read, "**...the voice of thy brother's blood crieth unto me from the ground.**" (Gen. 4:10)

Here the Bible teaches us that blood *cries out* to God when it's shed. And, in Hebrews 12:24, we read that the shed blood of Jesus Christ, "**...speaketh better things than** *that of* **Abel.**"

This clearly shows that the blood of Jesus Christ speaks to God on a sinner's behalf. This is just another reason why the blood of Jesus is so important!

Rose again. This refers to Christ's resurrection from the dead. And by raising from the dead by his own power, he proved that he had the power of eternal life.

The Bible further teaches that at Christ's ascension He took His blood to the third heaven and offered it up to God upon the mercy seat there.

We read this is Hebrews 9:12 and 24-26:

12 Neither by the blood of goats and calves, <u>but by his own blood he entered in once into the holy place</u>, having obtained eternal redemption *for us*... **24 For <u>Christ is not entered into the holy places made with hands</u>, which are the figures of the true; <u>but into heaven itself</u>, now to appear in the presence of God for us: 25 Nor yet that he should offer himself often, as the high priest entereth into the holy place every year with blood of others; 26 For then must he often have suffered since the foundation of the world: but now once in the end of the world hath he appeared to put away sin by the sacrifice of himself.**

This offered blood is still on the mercy seat in heaven today, waiting to wash (Rev. 1:5; 1 Juan 1:7) all those who receive God's salvation by faith (Eph. 2:8,9) in the blood (Rom. 3:25).

According to the scriptures. The Gospel ends with these oh so important words! For, how can we help but think of all the Old Testament sacrificial lambs dying for the innocent—shedding their blood to remit the sins of others? These were all types pointing to Christ's one effectual sacrifice on the cross.

We also must remember the hundreds of prophecies of Christ Jesus dying for our sins in our place found throughout the Old Testament.

For example, who can forget the prophetic words of Abraham in Genesis 22:8, "**...God will provide HIMSELF a lamb...**"

And the clear prophecy of Isaiah 53:4-6 shows us Christ crucified:

"Surely he hath borne our griefs, and carried our sorrows: yet we did esteem him stricken, smitten of God, and afflicted. But **he *was* wounded for our transgressions, *he was* bruised for our iniquities**: the chastisement of our peace *was* upon him; and with his stripes we are healed. All we like sheep have gone astray; we have turned every one to his own way; **and the LORD hath laid on him the iniquity of us all**."

And how can we forget to mention the beautiful wording of Leviticus 17:11 in the King James Bible which shows God's foreknowledge of His shedding His own blood for mankind? It states:

"**For the life of the flesh *is* in the blood: and I HAVE GIVEN IT TO YOU upon the altar** to make an atonement for your souls: for it *is* the blood *that* maketh an atonement for the soul."

Christ's substitutionary blood atonement is found throughout the entire Old Testament in type or in prophecy. And, so important was Christ's shedding of blood, that He prophecied thousands of years before what He would do to save mankind. He then fulfilled His promise, *according to the scriptures.*

Plainly, the blood of Jesus Christ is clearly found throughout the entire Gospel. As one old preacher said, *"If you don't preach the blood atonement, you don't preach the Gospel."*

This is why it's so important to preach the Gospel of Christ's shed blood to lost sinners, for there is no other way to be saved except THROUGH HIS BLOOD (Eph. 1:7)!

Salvation by Faith in the Blood

The Biblical means of salvation in the church age is by GRACE through FAITH. We see this clearly in the following verses:
For <u>by grace are ye saved through faith</u>; and that not of yourselves: *it is* the gift of God: Not of works, lest any man should boast. (Eph. 2:8,9)

By whom also <u>we have access by faith into this grace</u> wherein we stand, and rejoice in hope of the glory of God. (Rom. 5:2)

And that from a child thou hast known the holy scriptures, which are able to make thee wise unto <u>salvation through faith</u> which is in Christ Jesus. (2 Tim 3:15)

But <u>without faith *it is* impossible to please *him*:</u> for he that cometh to God must believe that he is, and *that* he is a rewarder of them that diligently seek him. (Heb. 11:6)

But the question must be asked, *"Faith in what?"* The answer is found in Romans 3:25-28:

25 Whom God hath set forth *to be* a propitiation <u>through faith in his blood</u>, to declare his righteousness for the remission of sins that are past, through the forbearance of God; 26 To declare, *I say,* at this time his righteousness: that he might be just, and the justifier of him which believeth in Jesus. 27 Where *is* boasting then? It is excluded. By what law? of works? Nay: but by the law of faith. 28 Therefore we conclude that a man is justified by faith without the deeds of the law.

Here we read that for a person to be saved, his faith <u>must</u> be in THE SHED BLOOD OF THE LORD JESUS CHRIST. A sinner must TRUST the blood atonement of Christ as sufficient to save his soul. This is why the blood of Christ is so important, FOR A SINNER CAN ONLY BE SAVED BY FAITH IN CHRIST'S SHED BLOOD!

A well-known Christian author in the 1800's writes the following about verse 25 in his commentary on Romans:

> *"The whole passage, which Olshausen happily calls 'the Acropolis of the Christian Faith,' is of SPECIAL IMPORTANCE. It teaches that we are justified in a manner which is entirely of grace, without any merit of our own; through or by means of faith, and on the ground of the propitiatory sacrifice of Jesus Christ... The part assigned to faith in the work of our reconciliation to God is that of an instrument; it apprehends or appropriates the meritous ground of our acceptance, the work or righteousness of Christ... Because we are said to be justified by faith, of which Christ is the object, by faith in his blood, by faith in him as a sacrifice... Faith in a sacrifice is, by the very force of terms, reliance on a sacrifice."* [11]

Here, *"through faith in his blood,"* is called THE ACROPOLIS OF THE CHRISTIAN FAITH. That's how important it is! It is THE FOUNDATION of the doctrine of salvation.

To trust the shed blood of Jesus Christ is to wholly trust in Christ Himself and his sacrificial atonement upon the cross for our sins. Further, when one TRUSTS the shed blood of Jesus, he *appropriates* Christ's finished work as the satisfactory grounds of his salvation. A sinner's RELIANCE upon the blood proves he's not trusting his own righteousness, but Christ's righteousness alone. In fact, he DELARES Christ's righteousness (Rom. 3:26) and is made JUST (Rom. 3:26) by his faith.

A 14th century Reformer says it clearly:

"*The Gospel...shows us the blood of Christ in order that, retaining it ever afresh in our memories, <u>we might base our faith upon it</u>, and thus we might live in confidence, sure of our justification, of our resurrection, and of eternal life.*" [12]

Clearly SALVATION IS ONLY THROUGH FAITH IN THE FINISHED WORK OF CHRIST on the cross— HIS SACRIFICE OF SHEDDING HIS OWN BLOOD to pay for man's ungodly sins. How important, then, is the shed blood of Jesus Christ! FOR WITHOUT FAITH IN IT, <u>NO</u> <u>ONE</u> CAN BE SAVED!

Those Who Preach Salvation by Faith in the Blood vs. Those Who Don't

From the time of the apostles till now, true Christians have preached salvation by grace through faith in the shed blood of Jesus Christ. They've carefully pointed lost sinners to Christ crucified, paying man's sin debt by His bloody sacrifice on Calvary, and salvation by trusting that meritous act.

But modern Christians as a whole have ceased from preaching the blood. Rather, they preach a water-downed gospel of *love* and *sharing*, and instead instruct sinners to come to God *"the best way they know how,"* rather than the BIBLICAL WAY of relying upon God's sacrificial blood atonement by faith.

Instead of pointing the lost to Christ on the cross, most soul winners omit the Gospel in it's entirety, coaxing a sinner to just *repeat a prayer*, or *commit his life to Christ*, or *ask Jesus to come into his heart*. But they forget one thing—ALL THESE CAN BE DONE WITHOUT THE SINNER TRUSTING WHOLLY UPON THE SHED BLOOD OF JESUS FOR SALVATION!

Because the Gospel of Christ's shed blood has been omitted so frequently in modern evangelism, most Christian's don't even think a sinner must know about the blood of Christ to be saved. I've personally heard many modernists say things like, *"A person doesn't have to understand the Gospel to get saved!"* Or, *"A person can get saved without even knowing what the Gospel is!"*

But what saith the scriptures? According to the following verses, a person must first HEAR the Gospel and then UNDERSTAND it before he can TRUST it to be saved:

13 For whosoever shall call upon the name of the Lord shall be saved. 14 How then shall they call on

him in whom they have not believed? and <u>how shall they believe in him of whom they have not HEARD? and how shall they hear without a preacher?</u> 15 And how shall they preach, except they be sent? as it is written, <u>How beautiful are the feet of them that preach the gospel of peace</u>, and bring glad tidings of good things! 16 But they have not all obeyed the gospel. For Esaias saith, Lord, who hath believed our report? 17 So then <u>faith *cometh* by HEARING, and HEARING by the word of God</u>. (Rom. 10:13-17)

<u>In whom ye also *trusted*, after that YE HEARD the word of truth, the gospel of your salvation</u>: in whom also after that ye believed, ye were sealed with that holy Spirit of promise. (Eph 1:13)

Howbeit many of them which <u>HEARD the word believed</u>; and the number of the men was about five thousand. (Acts 4:4)

Peter rose up, and said unto them, Men *and* brethren, ye know how that a good while ago God made choice among us, <u>that the Gentiles by my mouth SHOULD HEAR the word of the gospel, and believe.</u> (Acts 15:7)

Biblically, God says a sinner <u>must</u> hear the Gospel before he can believe. For, how can someone believe in something he has never heard? And how can a sinner trust the blood of Christ to save his soul, if he hasn't heard that it's the blood that he must TRUST IN to be saved?

Thus, religious modernists and apostate liberals of today are guilty of preaching a BLOODLESS GOSPEL, which teaches a man can be saved without even hearing or understanding the true Gospel. This is devious and anti-biblical. People don't get saved without faith in the blood! Nor can they trust in it if they haven't heard it preached!

This modernistic *gospel of omission* deceives sinners into thinking they are saved by something they do (i.e. *pray, ask, beg,* or *commit themselves*). But biblically, a person cannot be saved unless he turns from trusting his own righteousness (something he's done) to Christ's righteousness (His dying for us unworthy sinners).

The born again Spanish Reformer Juan de Valdez (1500-1541) said it well:

"The doctrine of justification is the necessary theological supplement to the doctrine of atonement, for without the justification of the sinner, the work of Christ would be void of any soteriological meaning... <u>to pretend to come to God with our own righteousness or works as a human contribution to complete the work of salvation would be to pronounce insufficient Christ's work</u>." [13]

To leave off preaching the blood of Christ and instead tell a person he must do something to be saved leaves a person thinking that his own righteousness is what saves him. But according to the word of God, a person can <u>never</u> be saved until he understands he can't save himself, and then, as a repentant sinner, comes to God trusting Him alone for salvation.

Romans 10:1-3 states this clearly:

"Brethren, my heart's desire and prayer to God for Israel is, that they might be saved. For I bear them record that <u>they have a zeal of God, but not according to knowledge. For they being ignorant of God's righteousness, and going about to establish their own righteousness, have not submitted themselves unto the righteousness of God.</u>"

Before a sinner can be saved, he must first *hear* the Gospel, *realize* that Christ died for his sins in his place, and *understand* that salvation is only by trusting the blood sacrifice of Christ, for this is the only way to submit one's self to the righteousness of God!

Sadly, Modern Christianity has departed from this Biblical truth, when it preaches that salvation is by *repeating a prayer* (i.e. the Sinner's Prayer). But what if a person REPEATS a prayer without REPENTING from the heart, and without RELYING UPON the blood of Jesus Christ for salvation? Is he saved? No!

Jesus speaks of such people in Matthew 15:8, "**This people draweth nigh unto me with their MOUTH, and honoureth me with *their* lips; but their HEART is far from me.**"

Clearly salvation is a heart thing. A person must TRUST the blood sacrifice of Christ from his HEART to be saved. It's what he trusts in from the heart (the blood of Christ) that saves him, not what he says from his MOUTH.

Dr. John R. Rice in his pamphlet "What Must I do to be Saved?" makes this very plain:

> "*Many people believe that a sinner cannot be saved without a period of prayer, without consciously calling upon God* [from the mouth]. *However, the Bible does not say that a sinner must pray in order to be saved.* In fact, immediately following the verse in Romans 10:13 is an explanation which shows that *calling on God is an evidence of faith in the heart and that it is really faith which settles the matter*...*No matter how long he prays, if he does not trust in Christ, he can never be saved. If he trusts in Christ without conscious prayer, then he is saved already. There is just one plan of salvation and just one step a sinner must take to secure it. That step is to believe on the Lord Jesus Christ!*"

Jesus makes it very clear in Matthew 13:15, speaking of the Pharisees, that salvation or conversion is FROM THE HEART:

"For this people's heart is waxed gross, and *their* ears are dull of hearing, and their eyes they have closed; lest at any time they should see with *their* eyes and hear with *their* ears, and should <u>understand with *their* heart</u>, and <u>should be converted</u>, and I should heal them."

Today's *Bloodless Christianity* has then become Phariseeical in its teachings and actions. Not only does it omit the important, soul-saving blood of Jesus Christ in its modernistic plan of salvation, but it also closes its eyes and ears to the truth of the Gospel—that salvation is by heartfelt faith in the blood of Jesus.

So ingrained in the minds of modern Christians is the teaching that a man can be saved apart from the blood of Christ, that I've even had several Independent Baptists attempt to call me a *heretic* for preaching that salvation is only by faith in the blood of Christ. One even going so far as to say that preaching salvation by faith in the blood is "*a new fangled Gospel.*"

Yet, the truth is that apostate Christianity has departed from *the old time way* of preaching *the old slaughter house religion* and *they* are the ones preaching a *new apostate gospel*—a Gospel without blood.

The Bible speaks of the church in the last days as Laodicea. In Revelation 3:15-19, God says of this church:

"**I know thy works, that thou art neither cold nor hot: I would thou wert cold or hot. So then because thou art lukewarm, and neither cold nor hot, I will spue thee out of my mouth. Because thou sayest, I am rich, and increased with goods, and have need of** nothing; and knowest not that <u>**thou art wretched, and miserable, and poor, and blind, and naked**</u>**: I counsel thee to buy of me gold tried in the fire, that thou mayest be rich; and white raiment, that thou mayest be clothed, and** *that* **the shame of thy nakedness do not appear; and <u>anoint thine eyes with eyesalve, that thou mayest see.</u> <u>As many as I love, I rebuke and chasten: be zealous therefore, and repent.</u>**"

Could it be that the reason that God is angry with the Laodicean church is because it has left off preaching the blood of Christ as the only means of salvation? I submit to you that this is the very reason that God is sickened!

Laodicea is spiritually blind, and has closed its eyes to the truth of the Gospel. Instead of pointing others to Christ, the Church only speaks of itself, bragging upon it's riches. It preaches the Laodicean Gospel of man's PROSPERITY instead of Christ's PROPITIATION. For this reason God commands it to REPENT!

Probably the most popular Laodicean Gospel is that of telling a sinner to simply *ask Jesus into his heart*. But where is this found in the Bible? It's simply not there. How could a soul be saved by ASKING FOR FORGIVENESS, without TRUSTING in the finished work of Christ TO BE FORGIVEN?

To ask God for forgiveness, outside of trusting the blood, is to ask God to die all over again to pay for your sins! But to trust Christ's sacrifice on Calvary is to rely upon His finished work as sufficient to save you! Then and only then will Jesus enter a sinner's heart.

We see this in Ephesians 3:17: "**That <u>Christ may dwell in your hearts by faith</u>; that ye, being rooted and grounded in love.**"

Jesus doesn't enter anyone's heart just because he *asks*. Rather, Jesus only enters a person's heart when that person's complete *faith* is in His finished substitutionary blood atonement.

Christianity didn't always omit the blood atonement of Jesus. For more than 1800 years, saints of God were faithful in preaching salvation by FAITH IN THE BLOOD of the Lord Jesus Christ. (That's why most of them were killed!)

From the times of the apostles to the times of the Reformation, until today, history shows literally millions of ministers preaching the blood of Christ as the only means of redemption, and against a religious works-based setup.

It's only been in the last several hundred years that Christianity as a whole has turned from preaching *reliance* upon THE BLOOD SACRIFICE to preaching a *ritualistic* BLOODLESS SUBSTITUTE (i.e. commit your life to Christ, invite him into your heart, repeat a prayer, etc).

Let us look at some famous quotes of well-known Christians who preached salvation by Christ's bloody sacrifice to prove that "TRUST THE BLOOD" is not a "*new fangled Gospel,*" but rather *the old time Gospel* of the Apostles.

Spanish Reformer Cassidoro de Reina wrote the following in his confession of Faith in 1560:

"*The which dying in the flesh, death of the cross, and being buried and risen again the third day from the dead by his own power...and in his name was preached to all the world...the remission of sins to all believers...This we understand to be that New Testament that God had promised his people, ratified and made firm for ever with the death of our Lord Jesus Christ, and with his shedding of blood; that is by another name as known to us as the Gospel.*"

"*By this confession we renounce all human merit or satisfaction that is taught to make one able to reach forgiveness of sins outside of the merit and satisfaction that the Lord has done for all of us that trust in him...there is no other way for a man to be justified, saved,* admitted into the alliance of the New Testament...*for the merit and efficacy of Him who has given us forgiveness and imputed his righteousness and innocence...*"

In 1602, Cipriano de Valera, another Spanish reformer wrote the following words in the preface of his Spanish Bible revision:

"Because it is not right to conform the certain with the uncertain, the word of God with the word of men...I again plead to our good merciful God and Father that He give you grace to hear Him and to know His will and that knowing it you will conform to it. And so be saved through the blood of the Lamb without blemish that sacrificed himself on the altar of the cross to forgive our sins before God. Amen. So be it."

And again in 1588 in his tract *Dos Tratados*, Valera wrote the powerful words:

"In as much as Purgatory, we say that there is no other Purgatory than the blood of Christ, that purged our sins by whose purgation we are reconciled with the eternal Father."

Charles Hodge, D.D., in his Commentary on the book of Romans wrote the following in the 1800's, *"The most obvious construction is that adopted in our version [the KJV], as well as in the Vulgate, and by Luther, Calvin, Olshausen and many others, 'through faith in his blood' so that the blood of Christ, as a propitiatory sacrifice, is the ground of the confidence expressed in* πιστος (faith)."

Further Mr. Hodge states, in speaking of Romans 3:25, *"This clause contains the ground of our deliverance from the curse of the law, and of our acceptance with God, and <u>constitutes therefore... the apostles exhibition of the plan of salvation.</u>"*

The Only Biblical plan of salvation is TRUST THE SHED BLOOD OF JESUS CHRIST TO BE SAVED!

Rev. Dr. Winslow of Bath says it this way:

"God does not accept you on the ground of a broken heart—or a clean heart—or a praying heart... <u>He accepts you wholly and entirely on the ground of the ATONEMENT of His blessed Son. Cast yourself, in childlike faith, upon that atonement—Christ dying for the ungodly, (Rom. 5:6), and you are saved!</u>"

And who can forget the famous Baptist Charles Hadden Spurgeon? Time and again he preached salvation by faith in the blood, and cried aloud against those apostates in his time who tried to make salvation dependent upon what a man does. Below are some of his most powerful quotes on the subject:

"<u>We shall preach of the sprinkled blood, and of Jesus the great sacrifice for sin</u>; and then we shall press upon all who know the value of the great redemption that they teach the young in their earliest days what is meant by the death of Jesus and <u>salvation through his blood</u>."

"<u>Woe unto the man that tramples upon the blood of Christ, and treats it as an unholy thing! Alas! I fear that many are doing so at this hour, not only among the outside world, but among those who profess and call themselves Christians.</u>"

"*He that will not accept the propitiation which God hath set forth must bear his own iniquity...If you come before God without the atoning blood, you have neither part nor lot in the matter of the covenant inheritance, and you are not numbered among the people of God.*"

"*Brethren, I do not think a man ought to hear a minister preach three sermons without learning the doctrine of the atonement...I would desire never to preach at all without seting forth salvation by faith in the blood of Jesus...it will disgust the enemy, but it will delight the faithful.* Substitution seems to be to be the soul of the gospel, the life of the gospel, the essence of the gospel; therefore must it ever be in the front.*"

"*Certain vainglorious minds are advancing—advancing from the rock to the abyss. They are making progress from truth to falsehood.* They are thinking, but their thoughts are not God's thoughts, neither are their ways his ways. *They are leaving the gospel, they are going away from Christ, and they know not whither. In quitting the substitutionary sacrifice they are quitting the sole hope of man.*" (pg 16) [11]

And again in his sermon Our Suffering Substitute, Spurgeon says, "*Thou art to be saved by faith in Christ...and in Christ alone.* Do not think thou must experience this, or that, before thou comest unto Jesus...*Rely not on anything thou canst DO, or THINK, or SAY, or know; rest alone on Jesus only, and thou art saved. Give up all other trusts, and rely on Jesus alone, alone on Jesus, and thou shalt pass from death unto life.*"

The words of William Reid, are likewise very powerful:

"The gospel is the report of a peace purchased by the BLOOD OF CHRIST for poor sinners... The Gospel of the grace of God does not consist in pressing the duty defined by the words, 'Give your hearts to Christ,' although that is often unwisely pressed upon inquirers after salvation as if it were the gospel; but the very essence of the gospel is contained in the words, 'Having liberty to enter into the holiest BY THE BLOOD OF JESUS...'

The true gospel is: Accept the free gift of salvation from wrath and sin by receiving Jesus Himself, and all the benefits He purchased 'WITH HIS OWN BLOOD...' 'THE BLOOD OF JESUS' is the ground of peace with God to every believing sinner below, and it will be the subject of the everlasting song of the redeemed above.

Awakened sinner! Begin at the beginning of the alphabet of salvation, by looking upon Him who was pierced on Calvary's cross for our sins–look to the Lamb of God, and keep continually looking unto Jesus, and not at your repentings, resolutions, reformation, praying, reading, hearing, or anything of yours as forming any reason why you should be accepted, pardoned, and saved–and you will soon find peace... There is no other way of being saved but by the blood of Christ..." [15]

Finally, Rev. T.T. Martin (1862-1939) wrote the following in his book God's Plan With Men:

"If you are trusting anything other than Jesus Christ and His shed blood, then according to the Bible, you are not saved. If you are trusting Jesus Christ plus something else, then you are not saved. We cannot

trust our morality, our good works, or reformation or anything else. We must trust Christ and Him alone."

These are just some of the many millions of faithful ministers who unwaveringly preached FAITH IN THE BLOOD OF CHRIST as the only means of salvation. To them, the blood of Jesus Christ was important!

Thus, it must dogmatically be stated, *"Biblically, anyone who preaches that salvation is by any other means than by faith alone in the finished work of Christ—His shed blood—is a liar and an apostate, and is nothing more than a tool of Satan to deceive and damn souls to hell with a false plan of salvation!"*

CHAPTER THREE
THE POWER OF THE BLOOD

In our first chapter we looked at what blood is, and how its very existence proves there is a Creator who gave us life.

In our second chapter we learned that blood sacrifice is the only thing that remits sin and brings forgiveness, and that salvation is only obtained by faith in the shed blood of Jesus Christ on Calvary.

Now let us turn our attention to what the blood does according to the Bible. For the effectual power of the blood shows just how important it is!

The Atoning Power of the Blood

Throughout the entire Old Testament, God spoke to Israel of ATONEMENT. And this atonement could only be made through the shedding of blood. In Leviticus 17:11 we read:

"For the life of the flesh *is* in the blood: and I have given it to you upon the altar to make an atonement for your souls: for <u>it *is* the blood *that* maketh an atonement for the soul</u>."

The word *atonement* means *"Expiation; satisfaction or reparation made by giving an equivalent for an injury, or by doing or suffering that which is received in satisfaction for an offense or injury."* [16]

The word *atonement* broken up in syllables is AT-ONE-MENT. Biblically, for a sinner to be *at one* with God, or no longer at odds with Him, he must have a sacrifice made on his behalf. In the Old Testament, God accepted the sacrifice of a lamb.

However, no longer is the sacrifice of an animal needed, for God himself—the Lord Jesus Christ—died on the cross of Calvary, shedding *His own blood* for us. He is the SACRIFICAL BLOOD ATONEMENT, man's only way to God!

The apostle Paul, speaking to the Christians in Rome, says the following in Romans 5:11, "**...But we also joy in God through our Lord Jesus Christ, by whom we have now received the atonement.**"

Have you, dear reader, accepted the ATONING blood of Christ as *satisfactory* to save your soul and bring you to God? For without Christ's atonement on the cross, you cannot even come to God.

The Reconciling Power of the Blood

In John 3:36 we read: "**He that believeth on the Son hath everlasting life: and he that believeth not the Son shall not see life; but the wrath of God abideth on him.**"

Here, we find that God's wrath abides upon all sinners who reject Jesus Christ and His atoning sacrifice for sins. This is why man needs to be reconciled.

Speaking of RECONCILIATION in 2 Cor. 5:18-21, the apostle states:

> "**And all things** *are* **of God, who hath reconciled us to himself by Jesus Christ, and hath given to us the ministry of reconciliation; To wit, that <u>God was in Christ, reconciling the world unto himself</u>, not imputing their trespasses unto them; <u>and hath committed unto us the word of reconciliation</u>. Now then <u>we are ambassadors for Christ, as though God did beseech</u> *<u>you</u>* <u>by us: we pray</u> *<u>you</u>* <u>in Christ's stead, be ye reconciled to God</u>. For he hath made him** *to be* **sin for us, who knew no sin; that we might be made the righteousness of God in him.**"

Here Paul is speaking to the Christians in Corinth, and he tells them that Christ Jesus did all that is necessary to reconcile the world unto himself. However, a person who is still not born again (saved), must avail himself of Christ's atoning sacrifice, and thereby be reconciled to God by trusting the shed blood of Jesus Christ. This is why there is the *ministry* of reconciliation.

Colossians 1:20,21 further shows us that it's the blood alone that makes peace or reconciliation with God:

"**And, <u>having made peace through the blood of his cross, by him to reconcile all things unto himself</u>; by him,** *I say,* **whether** *they be* **things in earth, or things in heaven. <u>And you, that were sometime alienated and enemies in</u>** *<u>your</u>* **<u>mind by wicked works, yet now hath he reconciled</u>.**"

Paul here is speaking to those Christians in Colosse who have trusted Christ as their Saviour. Those who have accepted Christ's sacrifice by FAITH IN IT are *those* who are reconciled! How about it dear reader, are you yet reconciled to God through the blood of Jesus Christ? Have you trusted His sacrifice as sufficient to save you? Christ has done all that's necessary, now you must trust Him in order to be reconciled to God.

The Redeeming Power of the Blood

The powerful blood of Jesus also REDEEMS, as we see in the following verses:

"**In whom we have <u>redemption through his blood</u>, the forgiveness of sins, according to the riches of his grace.**" (Eph. 1:7)

"**In whom we have <u>redemption through his blood</u>,** *even* **the forgiveness of sins.**" (Col. 1:14)

"Forasmuch as ye know that <u>ye were not redeemed with corruptible things</u>, *as* silver and gold, from your vain conversation *received* by tradition from your fathers; <u>But with the precious blood of Christ</u>, as of a lamb without blemish and without spot." (1 Peter 1:18,19)

"Neither by the blood of goats and calves, but <u>by his own blood he entered in once into the holy place, having obtained eternal redemption *for us.*</u>" (Heb. 9:12)

Redemption means to *buy back* or *purchase something*. The best way to illustrate this is the story told years ago of a young boy who lost his small boat. He had spent several years carving this beloved toy from wood, and one day decided he'd launch it in a creek of running water. Upon placing his boat upon the water, the swift-running current carried his ship off in the distance and out of sight. The boy cried for days upon the loss of his precious creation, but to no avail. However, a few days later, a classmate told him of finding a small vessel. When he showed it to the boy he cried, *"That's my lost ship!"*

The classmate, unwilling to part empty-handed, would not relinquish the toy without a price. So the rightful owner bought the toy for a few dollars. As he walked home, he repeated to himself, *"You're mine little boat! You're mine twice! I made you and I bought you. You're mine twice!"*

How greatly this illustrates Biblical salvation! God created man, but through his sin, man became lost with no way back to his Maker. For this, God willingly died on the cross, paying for man's sin in order to bring him back to Himself. He bought and purchased the souls of mankind with His own blood (Acts 20:28).

Through Christ, salvation is PAID IN FULL! And forgiveness is offered to all who receive Christ as their Saviour.

Those who receive Jesus by faith in His blood (the purchase price of their redemption) are then redeemed or bought back. And just like that little boy and his boat, God says to all saved sinners, *"You are now mine! You are mine twice! I made you and I bought you with my own precious blood!"*

How important is the redeeming power of the blood of Jesus Christ, for without it, man is lost in the sea of sin with no way back to his Creator!

The Cleansing Power of the Blood

Not only does the blood of Christ Jesus reconcile, redeem and atone, but it also cleanses and washes away man's sin. We see this in the following verses:

"...**the blood of Jesus Christ his Son cleanseth us from all sin.**" (1 John 1:7b)

"...**Unto him that loved us, and washed us from our sins in his own blood.**" (Rev. 1:5b)

How important then is the blood of Jesus Christ, for without it no one could ever appear spotless before God! The blood is the only thing that can wash man's sins away.

The old Hymn states it well, *"What can wash away my sins? Nothing but the blood of Jesus!"*

The blood of Christ is also called PURGING BLOOD in Hebrews 9:14: "**How much more shall the blood of Christ, who through the eternal Spirit offered himself without spot to God, purge your conscience from dead works to serve the living God?**"

So powerful is the blood of Jesus, that a sinner can even have his dirty conscience cleansed by it!

How about it reader, are you a blood-washed child of God? Have you been to Jesus for the cleansing fount, are you washed in the blood of the Lamb?

The Sanctifying Power of the Blood

"Wherefore Jesus also, that he might sanctify the people with his own blood, suffered without the gate." (Heb. 13:12)

This verse states that the reason Jesus suffered and died, was to SANCTIFY those who trust Him as Saviour.

Sanctify means to *make holy, to set apart, to purify.*[17] Man of himself is not holy, rather wicked, with a sinful nature. Thus, the only way to be made holy in the sight of God and be set apart from hell deserving sinners is through the blood of Jesus Christ!

Almost all the world's man-made religions were founded with the intention of purifying or making man holy. Yet they try to attain holiness without the blood of Christ. They sanctify themselves through holy water, self-chastisement, vain repetitions and more. But no matter how hard they meditate or how much they set themselves apart from sin, they can never be holy enough in their own righteousness to obtain heaven. They still have a sinful nature, and all their righteousnesses are as filthy rags in God's eyes (Isa. 64:6).

However, through the blood of Jesus Christ, God Himself purifies the sinner, giving him *a new nature and a new heart* (Ezek. 36:26). A saved person is then called *a new creature* (2 Cor. 5:17), set apart to live a holy life to please and honor Him who loved him enough to die for him.

How about you? Have you been sanctified by the blood of Jesus Christ?

The Justifying Power of the Blood

The blood of Jesus also JUSTIFIES. Justification is a judicial term, which according to Webster's 1828 dictionary means *"to absolve from merited punishment... and to accept as righteous on account of the merits of the Saviour."* [18]

When a person accepts Jesus Christ as his Saviour, he immediately receives absolution or forgiveness of his sins.

We see this not only in the dictionary, but in breaking up the syllables of the word JUSTIFIED. When I personally accepted Jesus Christ, the Bible tells me that in God's eyes it's *JUST-IF-I'D* never sinned!

Morever, God imputes His righteousness to a sinner who comes to Him by faith in His blood. We read of imputed righteousness in Romans 4:2-8:

2 For if Abraham were justified by works, he hath *whereof* to glory; but not before God. 3 For what saith the scripture? Abraham believed God, and it was counted unto him for righteousness. 4 Now to him that worketh is the reward not reckoned of grace, but of debt. 5 <u>But to him that worketh not, but believeth on him that justifieth the ungodly, his faith is counted for righteousness.</u> 6 <u>Even as David also describeth the blessedness of the man, unto whom God imputeth righteousness without works</u>, 7 *Saying,* Blessed *are* they whose iniquities are forgiven, and whose sins are covered. 8 <u>Blessed *is* the man to whom the Lord will not impute sin.</u>

Man cannot get to heaven by his works. God will never accept what man does to justify himself before God. The only way God will ever accept a sinner, is if that sinner accepts the blood sacrifice of Jesus Christ as sufficient to save his soul.

When a sinner is saved, according to the above passage, he is *forgiven* (vs 7), *covered* (vs 7), *blessed* (vs 6), *justified* (vs 5) and *imputed God's righteousness* (vs 6).

How important then is the blood of Jesus Christ, for faith in it is the only way a sinner can be MADE RIGHTEOUS in God's eyes!

Another important note is that JUSTIFICATION is said to be by three things in the book of Romans:

Being justified freely by his GRACE through the redemption that is in Christ Jesus. (Rom 3:24)

Therefore we conclude that a man is justified by FAITH without the deeds of the law. (Rom 3:28)

Much more then, being now justified by his BLOOD, we shall be saved from wrath through him. (Rom 5:9)

Thus, as we've seen time and again in the Bible, THE ONE AND ONLY WAY TO BE JUSTIFIED, (forgiven of all sins and imputed God's righteousness) IS BY GOD'S GRACE THROUGH OUR FAITH IN THE BLOOD OF JESUS CHRIST!

This is how important the blood is, for without trusting the blood of Jesus Christ, a sinner can never be JUSTIFIED, given God's imputed righteousness or be SAVED from wrath (Hell).

Are you trusting solely in the blood of Jesus Christ for salvation? For justification comes only through trusting the blood.

The Propitiatory Power of the Blood

The word *propitiation* literally means *the act of appeasing wrath*. It comes from the word *propitiate*, which means *to appease one offended and render him favorable; to make propitious.* [19]

God is angry with man's sin, but because He is a gracious and merciful God, He sent His son Jesus to die as the Propitiation for the sins of the whole world. We read this in the following verses:

And he is the propitiation for our sins: and not for ours only, but also for *the sins of* the whole world.
(1 John 2:2)

Herein is love, not that we loved God, but that he loved us, and sent his Son *to be* the propitiation for our sins.
(1 John 4:10)

Jesus Christ's blood sacrifice is the propitiatory act of APPEASING God's wrath on sin. And only through the shed blood of the Lord Jesus Christ are man's offenses forgiven and man is made favorable in God's sight.

Further, Romans 3:25 tells us that the only way a sinner can make Jesus his Propitiation is through faith in the blood:

Whom God hath set forth *to be* a propitiation through faith in his blood, to declare his righteousness for the remission of sins that are past, through the forbearance of God. (Rom. 3:25)

Is your faith, dear reader, in the all important propitiatory shed blood of Jesus Christ?

Victory Through the Blood

"And they overcame him by the blood of the Lamb, and by the word of their testimony; and they loved not their lives unto the death." (Rev. 12:11)

In this verse, we find those who have OVERCOME Satan through the blood of Jesus Christ.

The Bible calls the Devil *the accuser* (Rev. 12:10). And he rests not, accusing man of sin day and night before the throne of God. But when a sinner comes to God for salvation and accepts Christ's blood atonement by faith, he is immediately forgiven and his soul is washed in the precious blood of Jesus Christ. At this moment, Satan has no more power to accuse him of sin, for in God's eyes the sinner is now righteous and just. My how powerful is the blood of Jesus!

A sinner's only victory in this life is the Blood of Jesus Christ. For it is only the blood of Jesus that brings victory over sin, hell, death, and the grave. Plus, when a sinner is saved, he not only is FORGIVEN of all his sins, but GIVEN eternal life.

We see this in the following verses:

That whosoever believeth in him should not perish, but have eternal life. For God so loved the world, that he gave his only begotten Son, that whosoever believeth in him should not perish, but have everlasting life. (John 3:15,16)

And this is the will of him that sent me, that every one which seeth the Son, and believeth on him, may have everlasting life: and I will raise him up at the last day. (John 6:40)

Verily, verily, I say unto you, He that believeth on me hath everlasting life. (John 6:47)

Jesus said unto her, I am the resurrection, and the life: he that believeth in me, though he were dead, yet shall he live: And whosoever liveth and believeth in me shall never die. Believest thou this? (John 11:25,26)

For the wages of sin *is* death; but <u>the gift of God *is* eternal life</u> through Jesus Christ our Lord. (Rom. 6:23)

And this is the promise that he hath promised us, *even* <u>eternal life</u>. (1 John 2:25)

And this is the record, that God hath given to us <u>eternal life</u>, and this life is in his Son. (1 John 5:11)

According to the Bible, the sacrificial shed blood of Jesus is so powerful, that it's the only thing that can give victory over death! This eternal life only comes through Jesus Christ and his atonement! Have you yet received victory and eternal life through the blood?

The Blood Absolves All Doubt

Finally, the blood of Jesus is so powerful, it can completely obliterate all doubts a sinner might have of where he'll go when he dies.

Many who claim to be Christians today say things like, "*I have doubts of my salvation at times,*" or "*I doubt my salvation on a regular basis!*"

However, a person who is completely trusting in the shed blood of Jesus Christ will not doubt if he is saved or not. For, doubt comes from wondering if a sinner DID ENOUGH to get saved. But salvation by trusting in the blood of Jesus proves that a sinner is not trusting something *he did to get saved*, rather in the fact that JESUS DID ENOUGH for him to save him.

Juan Valdez, the 14th century reformer says it best:

"*Were my salvation in my own hands, I might doubt, but since it is in the hands of God, who has predestinated me to eternal life, I have no cause either to fear or to doubt!*" [20]

When someone trusts the blood of Christ solely for salvation, his doubts are removed, for he's trusting God to save him and not in himself. Those who doubt usually are those who trust what *they do* instead of what *God did* for them.

To trust the blood means to trust Christ has done all that's needed to save you. It is to rely completely upon the finished work of Christ's bloody sacrifice on the cross!

Doubt is the opposite of faith. To doubt is to disbelieve something is true. And no where in the Bible do we find a Christian doubting whether he's saved. It's simply not there.

None of the apostles ever doubted they were saved. Just look at the confession of the apostle Paul in 2 Tim. 1:12: "**For the which cause I also suffer these things: nevertheless I am not ashamed: for I KNOW WHOM I HAVE BELIEVED, and AM PERSUADED that he is able to keep that which I have committed unto him against that day.**"

Paul did not doubt if God was capable of saving him or keeping him saved. He trusted God to complete His promise!

Further, Paul stated:

Nay, in all these things we are more than conquerors through him that loved us. For I am persuaded, that neither death, nor life, nor angels, nor principalities, nor powers, nor things present, nor things to come, Nor height, nor depth, nor any other creature, shall be able to separate us from the love of God, which is in Christ Jesus our Lord. (Rom. 3:37-39)

Notice Paul does not say, *"We are effectual doubters..."* Rather he said, *"We are more than conquerors!"*

This is important to note, as modern Christianity, which does not preach salvation by faith in the blood, teaches that it's healthy for Christians to doubt their salvation. They further state that the way to absolve doubt is to give a Christian *assurance* of his salvation. This assurance usually consists of a preacher or altar worker encouraging the sinner to repeat the Sinner's Prayer after them. Then the sinner is told that he is *assured* of heaven because he DID something (i.e. he REPEATED the prayer).

But what if a person does this without trusting the blood of Jesus? He is still not saved, and he is left with a *FALSE ASSURANCE* of salvation. People like this usually doubt their salvation continually thereafter and hardly ever come to a true assurance of salvation, because they trust their ACT of prayer instead of Christ Jesus' bloody ATONEMENT.

The Bible mentions the word ASSURANCE seven times. One of these times, in Isaiah 32:17, we read the following, **"And the work of righteousness shall be peace; and the effect of righteousness quietness and assurance for ever."**

Here the Bible states dogmatically that the work of righteousness is PEACE and the effect is ASSURANCE forever!

As we've already seen, when a soul trusts the blood of Jesus Christ, he is trusting in Christ alone to save him. When Jesus does so, the sinner is then given Christ's righteousness and has peace with God. And at this moment, a sinner then has assurance of salvation. He is assured he is saved, not because of what HE DID, but because of what JESUS DID FOR HIM. To doubt would be to call God a liar, or count Christ's sacrifice as invalid and insufficient to save.

The Bible tells us that assurance does not come from man, but rather from God and his word. For in 1 John 5:13, we read:

These things have I written unto you that believe on the name of the Son of God; that ye may know that ye have eternal life, and that ye may believe on the name of the Son of God.

Here the word of God says that a person may KNOW that he has eternal life. How can he know? Simple, by reading the things that are written unto him (the Bible).

A Christian which accepts Jesus Christ by faith in the blood, as it's written in the scriptures, will KNOW he is saved, for he came to God the Bible way!

Thus, how powerful is the blood of Jesus Christ! It eradicates all doubts! For the blood gives confidence of salvation!

Finally, the Apostle Paul said in Romans 1:16, "**...I am not ashamed of the gospel of Christ: for it is the power of God unto salvation to every one that believeth; to the Jew first, and also to the Greek.**"

We see then that the power of God unto salvation is the Gospel of Christ. And as we've seen in our previous chapter, the POWER of the Gospel is the precious SHED BLOOD of Jesus!

Do you doubt? Why not trust solely in the blood atonement of Christ, and see if this doesn't take all your doubt away?

IN CLOSING

From all the verses covered in this small booklet, it's easy to see why the blood of Jesus Christ is so important. For biblically, A PERSON CANNOT EVEN BE A CHRISTIAN WITHOUT TRUSTING THE BLOOD ATONEMENT OF JESUS CHRIST!

The doctrine of salvation by faith in the blood of Jesus is the foundation of Christianity! It's been called *"The Acropolis of the Christian Faith,"* and *"The Apostle's Plan of Salvation."* That's how important it is!

Yet there exists literally millions of people on the earth who call themselves *Christians*, who never mention the blood of Christ, nor do they trust in it alone to save them. They are *apostates* which have fallen away from the *apostles* teaching of salvation through a BLOOD ATONEMENT. Instead, they teach man can attain heaven by his own SELF-ACHEIVEMENT without trusting the blood of Christ. They have twisted the Gospel from relying upon what *God himself did* for man, into something *man himself does*.

The scriptures prophesied this would happen several thousand years ago. Just look at the following verses:

> **Now the Spirit speaketh expressly, that <u>in the latter times some shall DEPART FROM THE FAITH</u>, giving heed to seducing spirits, and doctrines of devils; speaking lies in hypocrisy; having their conscience seared with a hot iron. (1 Tim. 4:1,2)**

> **Let no man deceive you by any means: <u>for *that day* shall not come</u>, except there come A FALLING <u>AWAY</u> [apostasy] <u>first</u>, and that man of sin be revealed, the son of perdition. (2 Thes. 2:3)**

This know also, that <u>in the last days perilous times shall come. For men shall be **LOVERS OF THEIR OWN SELVES**,</u> covetous, boasters, proud, **BLASPHEMERS**, disobedient to parents, unthankful, unholy, Without natural affection, trucebreakers, false accusers, incontinent, fierce, despisers of those that are good. Traitors, heady, highminded, lovers of pleasures more than lovers of God; **HAVING A FORM OF GODLINESS, BUT DENYING THE POWER THEREOF** [the precious blood of Jesus Christ]: from such turn away. For of this sort are they which creep into houses, and lead captive silly women laden with sins, led away with divers lusts, Ever learning, and never able to come to the knowledge of the truth. (2 Tim. 3:1-7)

Preach the word; be instant in season, out of season; reprove, rebuke, exhort with all longsuffering and doctrine. **<u>FOR THE TIME WILL COME WHEN THEY WILL NOT ENDURE SOUND DOCTRINE</u>**; but after their own lusts shall they heap to themselves teachers, having itching ears; And **<u>THEY SHALL TURN AWAY THEIR EARS FROM THE TRUTH, and shall be turned unto fables.</u>** (2 Tim. 4:2-4)

Even in the times of the apostles we find apostates who denied the blood of Jesus, seeking to turn people from *the true faith*.

In Acts 13:8, we read, "**But Elymas the sorcerer (for so is his name by interpretation) withstood them, <u>seeking to turn away the deputy from the faith</u>.**"

And even the apostle Paul himself, before he was saved, confesses that he persecuted and sought to destroy the true faith, as evidenced by Galatians 1:23,24, "**But they had heard only, That <u>he</u> [Paul] <u>which persecuted us in</u>**

times past now preacheth the faith which once he destroyed."

Thankfully, Paul accepted Christ Jesus as his Saviour, and God made him the *apostle to the Gentiles* (Rom. 11:13), and *put him in trust with the Gospel of Christ's blood atonement* (1 Thes. 2:4).
Yet in Galatians 1:6 and 7, Paul warns us of others who desired to *pervert* the Gospel:

"I marvel that ye are so soon removed from him that called you into the grace of Christ unto another gospel: Which is not another; but there be some that trouble you, and would pervert the gospel of Christ."

Further in the book of Galatians Paul speaks of *spies* and *false brethren* who've entered the church in Jerusalem seeking to turn people from the true faith and put them under bondage to the law:

"1 Then fourteen years after I went up again to Jerusalem... 2 And I went up by revelation, and communicated unto them that gospel which I preach among the Gentiles, but privately to them which were of reputation, lest by any means I should run, or had run, in vain. 3 But neither Titus, who was with me, being a Greek, was compelled to be circumcised: 4 And that because of false brethren unawares brought in, who came in privily to spy out our liberty which we have in Christ Jesus, that they might bring us into bondage: 5 To whom we gave place by subjection, no, not for an hour; that the truth of the gospel might continue with you." (Gal. 2:1-5)

Such spies of Satan still exist in our day seeking to turn us from the blood of Christ, and ensnare us in a works-based salvation. But Paul's powerful words in Galatians 2:16 prove that justification is not by works, but rather by faith:

"**Knowing that a man is not justified by the works of the law, but by the faith of Jesus Christ,** even we have believed in Jesus Christ, that we might be justified by the faith of Christ, and not by the works of the law: **for by the works of the law shall no flesh be justified.**"

Paul calls those who accept a BLOODLESS GOSPEL, "foolish" and points them to Christ crucified and salvation by faith alone, in his following words in Galatians 3:1,2:

"**O foolish Galatians, who hath bewitched you, that ye should not obey the truth, before whose eyes Jesus Christ hath been evidently set forth, crucified among you?** This only would I learn of you, Received ye the Spirit by the works of the law, or by the hearing of faith?"

Who were those which tried to turn Christians away from the faith, and blaspheme the Gospel of Christ's shed blood? Mostly they were the *religious crowd* of lost Jews who taught salvation came by keeping the law, instead of by faith alone. We see their hatred toward God's atoning sacrifice in Acts 13:44,45:

"And the next sabbath day came almost the whole city together to hear the word of God. **But when the Jews saw the multitudes, they were filled with envy, and spake against those things which were spoken by Paul, contradicting and blaspheming.**"

Sadly, apostate Christians of our day have become nothing more than modern, self-righteous Pharisees, "**teaching for doctrines the commandments of men**" (Mt. 15:9).

Most modern Christians not only do not preach the all important blood of Jesus as the only means of salvation, but they willingly omit it! And by so doing, they themselves have become *blasphemers* of the blood and *enemies* of the Gospel, just like the Pharisees of old.

In Philippians 1:27,28 the Apostle Paul commands Christians to do the following, warning them of their *adversaries*:

"<u>**Only let your conversation be as it becometh the gospel of Christ**</u>**: that whether I come and see you, or else be absent, I may hear of your affairs, that ye stand fast in one spirit, with one mind** <u>**striving together for THE FAITH OF THE GOSPEL**</u>**; And** <u>**in nothing terrified by your adversaries**</u>**: which is to them an evident token of perdition, but to you of salvation, and that of God.**"

Modernists and liberal Religious leaders who don't preach the blood for salvation are <u>NOT</u> Christians. They are ADVERSARIES of Christ and His blood atonement. They have made the blood of Jesus of little importance, and trick others into thinking salvation can be obtained by something man can do. In short, they are religious but lost (just like the Pharisees of old).

The apostle Jude warns of us such people, and encourages true Christians to defend the faith:

"<u>**Beloved, when I gave all diligence to write unto you of the common salvation, it was needful for me to write unto you, and exhort**</u> *<u>you</u>* <u>**that ye should earnestly CONTEND FOR THE FAITH**</u> **which was**

<u>once delivered unto the saints. For there are certain men crept in unawares,</u> who were before of old ordained to this condemnation, <u>ungodly men, TURNING the grace of our God into lasciviousness, and DENYING the only Lord God, and our Lord Jesus Christ.</u>" (Jude 3,4)

Here we find religious pretenders who have crept into the church which DENY the Lord Jesus Christ and his blood atonement, TURNING God's grace into *lasciviousness.*

These God-deniers no longer CONTEND for the faith as commanded, but try to undermine and destroy it. In short, the blood of Jesus Christ is just not important to them.

Of this crowd, the word of God says:

<u>Of how much sorer punishment, suppose ye, shall he be thought worthy, who hath trodden under foot the Son of God, and hath counted the blood of the covenant...an unholy thing, and hath done despite unto the Spirit of grace?</u> For we know him that hath said, Vengeance *belongeth* unto me, I will recompense, saith the Lord. And again, The Lord shall judge his people. *It is* a fearful thing to fall into the hands of the living God. (Heb. 10:29-31)

These blood-denying Pharisees are nothing more than religious hypocrites who have changed the Gospel from TRUSTING IN WHAT GOD <u>DID</u> FOR MAN, to WHAT MAN CAN <u>DO</u> FOR GOD.

Their modernistic gospel, which omits the blood of Jesus, puts all the emphasis on *man's* WORKS instead of *Jesus* and His FINISHED WORK. And, this form of humanism always leads to the sin of downgrading the divine blood of Christ, trodding it under foot, and leaving it unimportant and unessential.

Sadly, not only is the blood of Jesus not important to modern religious people, but they are actively hostile towards it. For those who think they are saved by what *THEY DO*, rather than by faith in what *JESUS DID* are always angry with those who try to tell them that salvation is not of works lest any man should boast (Eph. 2:8,9), because telling a man that his works do not save him is to tell him he's not *GOOD ENOUGH* to get to heaven. The self-righteous hate to hear this.

But that's exactly what the Gospel teaches! For it shows that only Jesus was *GOOD* (as all men are sinners) and He did *ENOUGH* when he offered himself up on Calvary as the ultimate sacrifice for sins.

Thus, to preach the importance of the blood of Jesus Christ, one will always receive persecution from lost religious people who think they can save themselves by what they do.

When the Apostle Paul preached the Gospel, CONTENDING FOR THE FAITH (Jude 3), he received much persecution, according to his own testimony:

"**For yourselves, brethren, know our entrance in unto you, that it was not in vain: But even after that we had suffered before, and <u>were shamefully entreated, as ye know, at Philippi, we were bold in our God to speak unto you the gospel of God with much contention</u>. For our exhortation *was* not of deceit, nor of uncleanness, nor in guile: But as we were allowed of God to be put in trust with the gospel, even so we speak; not as pleasing men, but God, which trieth our hearts. For neither at any time used we flattering words, as ye know, nor a cloak of covetousness; God *is* witness: Nor of men sought we glory, neither of you, nor *yet* of others, when we might have been burdensome, as the apostles of Christ.**" (1 Thes. 2:1-6)

Notice Paul confesses when he preached the Gospel, it was not without much contention. He further states that someone shamefully entreated him for preaching it.

Sadly, in our apostate age, those who preach the true Gospel of faith in Christ's atoning blood (as Paul did) will also encounter much contention from the lost religious crowd, who holds the blood of Jesus Christ in contempt.

Let us close by looking at the words of Apostle Paul in 1 Corinthans 2:1-5:

> "**And I, brethren, when I came to you, came not with excellency of speech or of wisdom, declaring unto you the testimony of God. For <u>I determined not to know any thing among you, save Jesus Christ, and him crucified</u>. And I was with you in weakness, and in fear, and in much trembling. And my speech and my preaching** *was* **not with enticing words of man's wisdom, but <u>in demonstration of the Spirit and of power: That your faith should not stand in the wisdom of men, but in the power of God</u>.**"

Notice Paul preached the Gospel under *the power of the Holy Spirit*, pointing people to *Christ crucified*—a bleeding Saviour. This is exactly what's missing in our day. We need more ministers who are willing to preach the blood of Jesus Christ amidst a world of apostasy and sin!

Further, Paul states he preached in much weakness, fear, and trembling. What was he afraid of?

It's the author's belief that Paul was afraid of not making the blood of Jesus important enough to the lost sinner. He was afraid of not making the Gospel so clear that a sinner could understand that salvation isn't by trusting in what HE DOES HIMSELF, but by simple childlike faith in what JESUS CHRIST DID FOR HIM almost two thousand years ago when He shed His oh so important blood on the cross of Calvary to atone for man's sin.

With this, dear reader, how important is the blood of Jesus Christ to you? According to the Bible, it's very important, for without it, you cannot be SAVED, BORN AGAIN, REDEEMED, RECONCILED, JUSTIFIED, WASHED or SANCTIFIED. And without trusting the blood of Jesus Christ, you can never receive ETERNAL LIFE which only Jesus Christ offers as a free gift to all who accept Him by faith in His bloody sacrifice.

Have you trusted the important blood of Jesus Christ to save your soul? If not, why don't you right now? For the only thing a man can do that's not a work is believe (trust) in the blood of Christ.

If you were saved reading this booklet, or you have questions or comments. Please email me at:

Robertbreaker3@hotmail.com

Or you can mail me a letter through regular mail at:

Robert Breaker III
740 Mike Gibson Lane
Milton, Florida 32583

And please check out my website at:

www.rrb3.com

Other Works by the Same author:

What the Bible Says about Marriage, Divorce, and Remarriage

Biblical Study Notes on Various Topics for Bible Believers

Why I am more than Just a Fundamentalist!

A Brief History of the Spanish Bible

The History and Truth about the Spanish Bible Controversy

The Truth About the Modern Gomez Spanish Bible

The Spanish Bible and those Courageous Men behind its Inception

The "Heresy" of the Sinner's Prayer

Hey, Where's the Blood?

Why I am a Baptist

These works can be found at:

www.rrb3.com

ABOUT THE AUTHOR

Robert Ray Breaker III is a King James Bible Believing Independent Baptist. His father led him to the Lord on July 29, 1992 in Milton, Florida.

A few years later he enrolled in the Pensacola Bible Institute and graduated there in 1998 with a Bachelors of Divinity.

While attending Bible School, Robert pastored, Garcon Point Baptist Church for a short time.

Two weeks after graduation, Robert went to Honduras, where he eventually became a Missionary for seven years on the field, planting several churches.

Today Robert is a member of an Independent Baptist church in Monterrey, Mexico, and travels extensively throughout Central, South, and even North America fulfilling his God-called ministry as a Missionary Evangelist to the Spanish speaking people.

He also desires to reach his own English Speaking people in this day and age of apostasy, compelling them to return to the old time way, and stand firmly on the Biblical doctrines of **salvation***,* **sanctification***, and* **the holy scriptures***.*

Bro. Breaker also runs BREAKER PUBLICATIONS, a small printing ministry, focusing on printing good, sound, biblical literature.

Footnotes:

1. "Written In Blood," by Robert E. Coleman, copyright 1972 by Fleming H. Revell Company, pg 16.

2. "Chemistry of the Blood," by M.R. DeHaan, copyright 1943 by Zondervan Publishing House, pg 18-19.

3. "Chemistry of the Blood," by M.R. DeHaan, copyright 1943 by Zondervan Publishing House, pg 18.

4. "Atlantis: The Antediluvian World," by Ignatius Donnelly, copyright 1949 by Harper and brothers, pg167.

5. "The Analytical Hebrew and Chaldee Lexicon," by Benjamin Davidson, seventh edition reprint of original copyright 1848 published by Hendrickson Publishers, pg 7.

6. "A Practical Grammar of Basic Biblical Hebrew," by Laurence M. Vance, copyright 1997 by Vance Publications, pg 91.

7. "Chemistry of the Blood," by M.R. DeHaan, copyright 1943 by Zondervan Publishing House, pg 14.

8. "Chemistry of the Blood," by M.R. DeHaan, copyright 1943 by Zondervan Publishing House, pg 17.

9. "Chemistry of the Blood," by M.R. DeHaan, copyright 1943 by Zondervan Publishing House, pg 16.

10. "Written In Blood," by Robert E. Coleman, copyright 1972 by Fleming H. Revell Company, pg 27-28, footnote.

11. "Commentary on the Epistle to the Romans, by Charles Hodge, D.D., April 1974 reprint of 1886 edition by William B. Eerdmans Publishing Company, Grand Rapids, Michigan."

12. "Juan de Valdez, (from his commentary of Romans 8:31, pg 41), taken from book: Juan de Valdez: and the Origins of the Spanish Reformation, by Jose C. Nieto, 1970, Librairie Droz, S.A., pg. 312."

13. "Juan de Valdez: and the Origins of the Spanish and Italian Reformation, by Jose C. Nieto, 1970, Librairie Droz, S.A., pg. 320-321."

14. His Sermon "The Blood of Sprinkling and the Children," printed by the Chapel Library, 2603 W. Wright Street, Pensacola, FL, 32505, pg 2-16.

15. Quotes from William Reid's, The Blood of Jesus, written around 1863, published by Chapel Library, 2603 W. Wright St., Pensacola, FL 32505, pgs 6-22.

16. "Webster's 1828 Dictionary, CD ROM.

17. Ilid.

18. Ilid.

19. Ilid.

20. Juan Valdez, from his tract: Trattetelli, pg 73, English translation by Opuscules, pg 183, as found in the book Juan de Valdez: and the Orgins of the Spanish and Italian Reformation, by Jose C. Nieto, 1970, Librairie Droz, S.A., pg. 330.

Brought to you by:

740 Mike Gibson Lane
Milton, Florida 32583

www.rrb3.com

Made in United States
Orlando, FL
26 May 2023